FALLING OR BE FLAILING

FALLING OR BE FLAILING

EMBRACING YOUR JOURNEY OF GROWTH AND RESILIENCE

Authored by

NEERAJ SHARMA

Office No. 03, Guru Harkishan Nagar,
Paschim Vihar, Delhi, 110087
Website: www.authorlandselfpublishing.com
Email: publish@authorlandselfpublishing.com

First Published by Authorland Self Publishing 2023
Copyright © Neeraj Sharma 2023
All Rights Reserved.

Title: Falling or Be Flailing
Price: ₹499 | $14.99
ISBN: 978-81-963253-7-4

DEDICATION

This book is dedicated to all the brave souls who have dared to face life's challenges head-on, refusing to be defined by their failures and setbacks. It is for those who have experienced moments of doubt, uncertainty, and fear, yet have found the inner strength to rise above and embrace their journey of personal growth and resilience. To the ones who have stumbled and fallen, only to gather the courage to rise again, this dedication is for you. Your resilience in the face of adversity serves as a beacon of hope, reminding us that failure is not the end, but rather a stepping stone on the path to success. This dedication is a tribute to the resilience, strength, and unwavering spirit of every individual who has chosen to embrace their journey, fall, and rise again. You are the embodiment of the human spirit, and this book is dedicated to you.

CONTENTS

PREFACE

Welcome to "Falling or Be Flailing: Embracing Your Journey of Growth and Resilience." I am honored to embark on this transformative journey with you as we explore the art of embracing life's ups and downs with courage, resilience, and a renewed sense of purpose.

Life is a series of experiences, both exhilarating and challenging, that shape who we are and who we become. It is through the falls and flailing moments that we discover our true strength and potential. This book is a testament to the power of embracing every twist and turn along the way, knowing that it is in these moments that we find the opportunities for growth and personal transformation.

In these pages, you will find a wealth of insights, stories, and practical exercises designed to help you navigate the complexities of life with grace and resilience. We will delve into topics such as self-compassion, cultivating a growth mindset, embracing vulnerability, and finding joy and fulfillment in everyday life. Each chapter is an invitation to reflect, learn, and take action, empowering you to embrace your unique journey of falling and flailing.

As the author of this book, I have poured my heart and soul into its creation, drawing from my own personal experiences and the wisdom of countless individuals who have faced adversity and emerged stronger than ever. My hope is that the words within these pages inspire you, challenge you, and ignite a sense of possibility within your heart.

"Falling or Be Flailing" is not a roadmap with all the answers, but rather a guide that encourages self-exploration and empowers you to define your own path. It is my sincere belief that within you lies a wellspring of resilience, courage, and untapped potential. By embarking on this journey together, we can uncover the tools and strategies needed to face life's challenges head-on, embrace our falls, and transform our flailing moments into stepping stones toward personal and professional success.

I invite you to approach this book with an open mind and an open heart. Allow yourself to fully immerse in the stories, reflect on the exercises, and engage in the practices shared throughout. Embrace the wisdom and insights that resonate with you, and leave behind anything that does not align with your personal journey. This is your book, and it is meant to be a companion on your unique path toward growth and resilience.

I am grateful that our paths have crossed through the pages of this book. I am confident that within you lies the power to rise above any challenge, to find beauty in the falls, and to embrace the transformative journey of falling or be flailing.

May you find inspiration, encouragement, and guidance within these pages as you embark on your own journey of growth, resilience, and self-discovery. May this book be a source of light and empowerment, reminding you that you have the strength to rise, the courage to embrace vulnerability, and the capacity to transform your life in profound ways.

Let us begin this transformative journey together.

With gratitude and excitement,

Neeraj Sharma
Founder, Director & CEO
Authorland Self Publishing LLP

FOREWORD

By Yukti Sharma

In the grand tapestry of life, it is often the moments of falling that shape us the most. It is in those vulnerable moments of flailing, when the ground beneath us gives way, that we are afforded the opportunity to rise stronger, wiser, and more resilient than ever before. This is the essence of "Falling or Be Flailing," a book that invites us to embrace the beauty and transformative power of our falls.

In a world that often idolizes success and achievement, we can easily become discouraged by our own perceived failures. We fear the unknown, the uncertain path, and the potential for stumbling along the way. But what if, instead of avoiding falls, we chose to embrace them? What if we saw them not as setbacks, but as stepping stones on our journey of personal growth and self-discovery?

"Falling or Be Flailing" is a heartfelt exploration of the human experience, a guide that reminds us that falling is an inherent part of our journey. Through captivating stories, insightful reflections, and practical strategies, this book illuminates the path to resilience, courage, and personal transformation.

As I embarked on this remarkable journey within the pages of "Falling or Be Flailing," I was struck by the profound wisdom and authenticity that emanates from its words. The author fearlessly shares their own experiences of falling, allowing us to witness the raw vulnerability that accompanies these moments. In doing so, they create a safe space for readers to reflect on their own falls and to find solace in the shared human experience.

One of the remarkable aspects of this book is its celebration of the beauty found in our falls. Rather than shying away from the discomfort and uncertainty, the author invites us to lean into those moments with curiosity and courage. Through personal anecdotes and inspiring examples, we are reminded that our falls hold invaluable lessons, gifts that can only be received when we are willing to embrace the experience fully.

In a world that often places a premium on success, "Falling or Be Flailing" provides a refreshing perspective. It challenges societal norms and encourages us to redefine our relationship with failure. Through its pages, we learn that falling is not a sign of weakness, but an invitation to learn, grow, and discover the depths of our own resilience.

As I journeyed through the chapters of this book, I found myself inspired to reevaluate my own relationship with failure and to embrace the beauty that lies within my own falls. I was reminded that life's challenges are not meant to break us, but to mold us into the best versions of ourselves.

"Falling or Be Flailing" is a testament to the resilience of the human spirit. It serves as a guiding light for those navigating the complexities of life, offering solace and encouragement during times of uncertainty. It reminds us that in our falls, we find the courage to rise, the strength to face adversity, and the wisdom to embrace the beauty of our imperfect journey.

As you embark on this transformative journey within the pages of "Falling or Be Flailing," I encourage you to approach it with an open heart and mind. Allow yourself to be vulnerable, to reflect on your own falls, and to find inspiration in the stories and insights shared. May this book empower you to embrace the beauty of your own falls, to rise with courage, and to navigate life's challenges with resilience and grace.

Yukti Sharma
Author of "Publish Your Book and Make Money"

Embracing the Journey

In life, we all face challenges, setbacks, and moments of uncertainty. These experiences can leave us feeling disheartened, lost, and overwhelmed. However, it is in these very moments that we have the opportunity to rise above our circumstances and discover our inner strength. "Falling or Be Flailing: Embracing Challenges and Finding Strength in Adversity" is a book that explores the transformative power of embracing life's challenges and using them as stepping stones towards personal growth and success.

In this introductory chapter, we set the stage for the journey ahead. We invite readers to reflect on their own experiences and mindset towards challenges, encouraging them to adopt a new perspective. Instead of fearing or avoiding challenges, we invite readers to embrace them as opportunities for growth and self-discovery.

We delve into the concept of a growth mindset, which is the belief that our abilities and intelligence can be developed through effort, practice, and learning. By adopting a growth mindset, we empower ourselves to face challenges head-on, knowing that we have the capacity to learn, adapt, and overcome obstacles.

The chapter highlights the importance of shifting our perspective on adversity. Rather than viewing challenges as roadblocks, we encourage readers to see them as necessary stepping stones on the path to personal and professional development. By reframing challenges as opportunities for learning and growth, we can navigate through them with resilience and determination.

Moreover, we discuss the power of vulnerability and authenticity. It is through acknowledging our vulnerabilities and embracing them that we tap into our true strength. We encourage readers to cultivate self-compassion and self-acceptance, recognizing that it is okay to stumble and make mistakes along the way. Vulnerability becomes a catalyst for personal growth and deepening connections with others.

The introduction also emphasizes the importance of embracing failure as a stepping stone towards success. We debunk the notion that failure is something to be feared or avoided, but rather a natural part of the learning process. By reframing failure as an opportunity to learn, we can overcome the fear of failure and take courageous steps towards our goals.

Finally, we invite readers to embark on a journey of self-discovery and self-belief. By cultivating inner strength, self-confidence, and a strong sense of self-worth, we lay the foundation for resilience and success in the face of challenges. Through practical exercises and reflection prompts, readers are encouraged to explore their values, passions, and purpose, ultimately aligning their actions with their authentic selves.

The introduction sets the tone for the rest of the book, inspiring readers to embrace the journey of falling and flailing. It instills a sense of hope, resilience, and empowerment, reminding readers that they have the power to navigate through challenges and emerge stronger on the other side.

As readers delve into the subsequent chapters, they will find practical strategies, insights, and real-life examples that guide them on their path of growth and self-discovery. With each turn of the page, they will gain a deeper understanding of how to navigate life's challenges, find strength in vulnerability, and transform setbacks into stepping stones towards success.

"Falling or Be Flailing: Embracing Challenges and Finding Strength in Adversity" is not just a book; it is a roadmap for personal transformation. It empowers readers to face life's challenges with resilience, self-belief, and the knowledge that falling doesn't mean failure—it simply means an opportunity to rise again. So, let the journey begin, and may you discover the power within you to embrace challenges, find strength in adversity, and create a life filled with purpose and fulfillment.

CHAPTER ONE

Understanding the Nature of Challenges

RECOGNIZING THE INEVITABILITY OF CHALLENGES

Life is a journey filled with ups and downs, successes and failures, joys and sorrows. It is a tapestry of experiences that shape and mold us into who we are. In this chapter, we delve into the concept of recognizing the inevitability of challenges and the transformative power they hold.

Challenges are an inevitable part of the human experience. No matter who we are, where we come from, or what our goals may be, we will encounter obstacles along our path. It is essential to recognize this truth and embrace it, for it is in the face of challenges that we have the opportunity to grow, learn, and evolve.

Often, we tend to view challenges as negative occurrences, as roadblocks standing in the way of our success or happiness. However, a shift in perspective can help us see challenges as opportunities for growth and self-discovery. It is through overcoming these challenges that we develop resilience, strength, and wisdom.

By recognizing the inevitability of challenges, we free ourselves from the burden of unrealistic expectations. We understand that setbacks and obstacles are not signs of failure, but rather invitations to dig deeper, find new solutions, and tap into our inner resources. Challenges push us outside of our comfort zones and encourage us to explore our potential.

Moreover, challenges provide valuable lessons and teach us essential life skills. They reveal our strengths, highlight areas for improvement, and foster personal growth. Each challenge we encounter serves as a stepping stone on our journey, shaping us into more resilient, adaptable, and compassionate individuals.

Recognizing the inevitability of challenges also helps us develop a mindset of acceptance and flexibility. Instead of resisting or avoiding challenges, we can approach them with an open mind and a willingness to learn. We can cultivate a sense of curiosity and curiosity about how challenges can contribute to our personal and professional development.

Additionally, acknowledging the inevitability of challenges allows us to let go of the fear of failure. It is natural to feel apprehensive when facing unknown or difficult situations. However, understanding that challenges are a normal part of life helps us reframe failure as a valuable learning experience. We can view failures as stepping stones towards success, as opportunities to learn, pivot, and grow.

In embracing the inevitability of challenges, we also foster a sense of empathy and compassion towards others. Recognizing that everyone faces their own unique set of challenges encourages us to extend understanding and support to those around us. We can create a community of shared experiences, where individuals uplift and encourage one another on their respective journeys.

Ultimately, recognizing the inevitability of challenges empowers us to take control of our narratives. Instead of being defined by our challenges, we can become the authors of our own stories. We can embrace challenges as opportunities to create meaningful change, to overcome adversity, and to become the best versions of ourselves.

As we navigate through life's inevitable challenges, we must remember that we are not alone. Countless individuals have faced and overcome similar obstacles. Their stories of triumph and resilience serve as beacons of inspiration, reminding us of our own inner strength and capacity for growth.

In the chapters ahead, we will explore practical strategies, tools, and insights to help us navigate through the inevitable challenges that arise in various aspects of life. From personal relationships to career aspirations, we will uncover how to approach challenges with grace, resilience, and a growth mindset.

So, let us embark on this journey together, knowing that challenges are not roadblocks, but stepping stones on our path to personal and professional fulfillment. By recognizing the inevitability of challenges, we open ourselves up to a world of possibilities, growth, and transformation. Let us embrace the challenges that lie ahead, for they hold the potential to shape us into the individuals we aspire to be.

EMBRACING THE GROWTH MINDSET

In life, we often encounter situations that test our abilities, challenge our beliefs, and push us outside of our comfort zones. These moments of uncertainty and difficulty can either be viewed as setbacks or opportunities for growth. It is in this context that embracing a growth mindset becomes crucial.

The concept of a growth mindset, popularized by psychologist Carol Dweck, revolves around the belief that our abilities and intelligence are not fixed traits but can be developed through effort, perseverance, and learning. It is the belief that we can cultivate and expand our skills and talents with dedication and a willingness to embrace challenges.

When we adopt a growth mindset, we shift our focus from seeking validation and avoiding failure to seeking growth and embracing challenges. We understand that setbacks and obstacles are not indicators of our inherent abilities or worth, but rather opportunities to learn, improve, and develop resilience.

Embracing a growth mindset allows us to approach challenges with curiosity, optimism, and a willingness to learn. Instead of being discouraged by failure or setbacks, we see them as stepping stones on our journey towards mastery. We understand that making mistakes and facing obstacles are essential parts of the learning process.

Moreover, a growth mindset helps us develop a sense of self-belief and empowerment. When we believe that our abilities are not fixed, we free ourselves from the limitations of self-doubt and embrace the potential for growth and improvement. We become more willing to take risks, try new things, and step outside of our comfort zones.

With a growth mindset, we also become more resilient in the face of adversity. Rather than being defeated by challenges, we see them as opportunities to build our resilience muscle. We understand that setbacks are temporary and that we can bounce back stronger and more determined than ever before.

Furthermore, embracing a growth mindset fosters a love for learning and a desire for continuous improvement. We become lifelong learners, seeking knowledge and skills that can enhance our personal and professional lives. We are open to feedback, constructive criticism, and new perspectives, recognizing that they are invaluable sources of growth and development.

In embracing the growth mindset, we also cultivate a positive and empowering internal dialogue. We replace self-limiting beliefs and negative self-talk with empowering statements and affirmations. We reframe challenges as opportunities, setbacks as lessons, and failures as stepping stones towards success.

Embracing the growth mindset not only benefits our personal development but also extends to our interactions with others. We become more supportive and encouraging of the growth and success of those around us. We recognize that their achievements do not diminish our own, but rather inspire us to strive for our own growth and potential.

In the chapters ahead, we will explore practical strategies and techniques to embrace the growth mindset in various areas of life. From personal growth to career advancement, we will uncover how a growth mindset can transform our perspectives, enhance our abilities, and unlock our full potential.

So, let us embrace the growth mindset as we embark on this journey of personal and professional development. Let us cultivate a mindset of growth, resilience, and continuous learning. With a growth mindset, we can overcome challenges, achieve our goals, and become the best versions of ourselves. The power to grow and evolve is within us, waiting to be unleashed.

SHIFTING PERSPECTIVE ON ADVERSITY

Adversity is an inevitable part of life. It comes in various forms, such as setbacks, challenges, and unexpected obstacles. Our response to adversity plays a significant role in determining the outcomes we experience. By shifting our perspective on adversity, we can transform it from a negative force to a catalyst for growth, resilience, and personal development.

Adversity, at its core, presents us with an opportunity to learn and evolve. It tests our character, resilience, and problem-solving skills. Instead of viewing adversity as something to be avoided or feared, we can reframe it as a teacher—a valuable source of lessons and growth.

One of the fundamental shifts in perspective involves embracing adversity as a natural and necessary part of the journey. Instead of perceiving it as a sign of failure or inadequacy, we can recognize that it is through adversity that we grow and develop. Adversity challenges us to step out of our comfort zones, stretch our limits, and discover our true potential.

Moreover, shifting our perspective on adversity allows us to see the hidden opportunities within challenging situations. It prompts us to ask ourselves, "What can I learn from this experience? How can I grow stronger? What new possibilities can emerge?" By seeking the silver linings and lessons amidst adversity, we open ourselves up to transformative experiences and personal growth.

Shifting perspective also involves reframing failure as a stepping stone towards success. Failure is often seen as something to be feared and avoided. However, when we shift our perspective, we recognize that failure is not a reflection of our worth or abilities, but rather a valuable feedback mechanism. It provides us with insights into what works and what doesn't, guiding us towards improved strategies and approaches.

Furthermore, shifting perspective on adversity involves embracing a growth mindset. This mindset sees challenges as opportunities for learning, development, and mastery. Instead of viewing adversity as a roadblock, we approach it with curiosity, determination, and a belief in our ability to overcome. A growth mindset allows us to see setbacks as temporary and surmountable, enabling us to persevere in the face of adversity.

Additionally, shifting perspective on adversity invites us to focus on the lessons learned rather than dwelling on the pain or difficulties. Adversity provides us with invaluable experiences and wisdom that can shape our character, strengthen our resilience, and enhance our problem-solving abilities. By shifting our focus from the negative aspects of adversity to the growth and wisdom gained, we empower ourselves to move forward with greater clarity and strength.

Moreover, shifting perspective on adversity helps us develop a sense of gratitude and appreciation for the challenges we encounter. While it may seem counterintuitive, embracing gratitude for adversity allows us to see the transformative power it holds. Adversity builds resilience, fosters empathy and compassion, and deepens our understanding of ourselves and others. It is through adversity that we often discover our inner strength and resourcefulness.

In conclusion, shifting our perspective on adversity opens up a world of possibilities. It transforms adversity from an obstacle to an opportunity, from a setback to a stepping stone, and from a source of fear to a catalyst for growth. By embracing adversity as a natural part of life, reframing failure, adopting a growth mindset, focusing on the lessons learned, and cultivating gratitude, we empower ourselves to navigate through challenges with resilience, determination, and a sense of purpose. Let us embrace adversity as an invitation for growth and transformation, and discover the strength and resilience that lie within us.

CHAPTER TWO

The Power of Resilience

BUILDING RESILIENCE AS A KEY LIFE SKILL

Resilience is a powerful life skill that enables individuals to navigate through challenges, bounce back from setbacks, and adapt to change. It is the ability to withstand and recover from adversity, maintain a positive outlook, and continue moving forward despite obstacles. Building resilience is not only essential for overcoming difficulties but also for personal growth, well-being, and success in various areas of life.

One of the key aspects of building resilience is developing a strong mindset. Resilient individuals possess a mindset that embraces challenges as opportunities for growth and learning. They view setbacks as temporary and solvable, and they believe in their ability to find solutions and overcome obstacles. This mindset allows them to maintain a positive outlook, stay focused on their goals, and persevere through difficult times.

Another important element of resilience is having a support system. Building and maintaining positive relationships with family, friends, mentors, or support groups provides a crucial network of emotional support and encouragement. Having people to lean on during challenging times can help individuals feel understood, validated, and empowered. Supportive relationships provide a safe space to express emotions, seek guidance, and receive practical help when needed.

Additionally, resilience is fostered through self-care practices. Taking care of one's physical, emotional, and mental well-being is essential for building resilience. Engaging in activities that promote relaxation, stress reduction, and self-reflection, such as exercise, meditation, journaling, or pursuing hobbies, helps individuals recharge and maintain a positive mindset. Prioritizing self-care allows individuals to better cope with stress, enhance their problem-solving abilities, and approach challenges with a clear and focused mind.

Adopting a growth mindset is also crucial for building resilience. Embracing a belief that skills, abilities, and intelligence can be developed through effort and practice empowers individuals to see challenges as opportunities for growth. Rather than viewing failures as indicators of incompetence, a growth mindset allows individuals to see them as stepping stones towards improvement and mastery. This mindset fosters a sense of perseverance, optimism, and a willingness to learn from mistakes.

Furthermore, building resilience involves developing effective coping strategies. Individuals who are resilient have a repertoire of healthy coping mechanisms that they can rely on during difficult times. These strategies may include problem-solving skills, positive self-talk, seeking social support, seeking professional help when needed, and engaging in activities that promote relaxation and stress reduction. By utilizing these coping strategies, individuals can manage stress, regulate emotions, and maintain their overall well-being in the face of adversity.

Building resilience also requires embracing flexibility and adaptability. Life is full of unexpected changes, and being able to adapt to new situations and circumstances is crucial. Resilient individuals are open to change, willing to adjust their plans, and find creative solutions when faced with unexpected challenges. They understand that rigidity can hinder progress and that being adaptable allows for greater resilience and the ability to seize new opportunities.

In conclusion, building resilience is a key life skill that empowers individuals to navigate challenges, recover from setbacks, and thrive in the face of adversity. It involves developing a strong mindset, cultivating supportive relationships, practicing self-care, adopting a growth mindset, developing effective coping strategies, and embracing flexibility and adaptability. By building resilience, individuals enhance their ability to overcome obstacles, maintain a positive outlook, and continue moving forward towards their goals. Resilience is not only essential for personal well-being but also for success in various areas of life. With resilience as a guiding force, individuals can face life's challenges with strength, determination, and the confidence to overcome any obstacles that come their way.

CULTIVATING A POSITIVE MINDSET

A positive mindset is a transformative force that shapes our thoughts, emotions, and actions. It is the lens through which we view the world, influencing our perceptions, attitudes, and ultimately, our experiences. Cultivating a positive mindset is about intentionally shifting our focus towards optimism, gratitude, and a belief in our own abilities. It is a practice that can bring profound changes to our lives and unlock our true potential.

One of the key aspects of cultivating a positive mindset is becoming aware of our thoughts and learning to reframe them. Our thoughts have a tremendous impact on how we feel and how we interpret the world around us. By consciously choosing to focus on positive thoughts and reframing negative ones, we can rewire our brains to seek opportunities, embrace challenges, and find the silver linings in any situation. This shift in perspective allows us to approach life with a sense of optimism and resilience, even in the face of adversity.

Gratitude is another powerful tool in cultivating a positive mindset. Practicing gratitude involves intentionally recognizing and appreciating the blessings, big and small, that we encounter in our lives. It shifts our attention away from what may be lacking or challenging and redirects it towards the abundance and beauty that surrounds us. By fostering a grateful attitude, we cultivate a deeper sense of contentment, joy, and appreciation for life's blessings. This, in turn, enhances our overall well-being and enables us to navigate challenges with greater strength and perspective.

Believing in our own abilities and cultivating self-confidence is another essential aspect of a positive mindset. When we have faith in our capabilities, we approach challenges with a can-do attitude and a belief that we have what it takes to succeed. Self-confidence fuels our motivation, determination, and resilience, allowing us to persevere through obstacles and setbacks. By recognizing our strengths and celebrating our achievements, we build a foundation of self-assurance that empowers us to pursue our goals and dreams with unwavering belief.

Cultivating a positive mindset also involves surrounding ourselves with positivity and inspiration. The people we associate with, the media we consume, and the environments we spend time in significantly influence our mindset. By seeking out positive influences, such as supportive and uplifting relationships, motivational books, podcasts, and uplifting environments, we create an ecosystem that nourishes our positive mindset. Surrounding ourselves with positivity reinforces our belief in our own potential and fosters a mindset of possibility and growth.

Practicing mindfulness and staying present is another powerful tool in cultivating a positive mindset. Mindfulness is the practice of being fully present in the current moment, without judgment or attachment to the past or future. It allows us to appreciate the beauty of each moment, find joy in simple pleasures, and cultivate a sense of inner peace. By practicing mindfulness, we can quiet the noise of negative thoughts, reduce stress, and cultivate a deep sense of gratitude and contentment.

In conclusion, cultivating a positive mindset is a transformative journey that empowers us to shape our lives according to our desires and aspirations. It involves shifting our focus towards optimism, practicing gratitude, believing in our own abilities, surrounding ourselves with positivity, and staying present through mindfulness. By cultivating a positive mindset, we unlock the power within us to overcome challenges, embrace opportunities, and live a life filled with purpose, joy, and fulfillment. Remember, a positive mindset is not about ignoring the realities of life, but rather about approaching them with a mindset that empowers us to navigate them with strength, resilience, and a belief in our own limitless potential.

DEVELOPING COPING MECHANISMS FOR RESILIENCE

Life is filled with ups and downs, challenges and triumphs. In order to navigate the inevitable hardships and setbacks that come our way, it is crucial to develop coping mechanisms that promote resilience. Coping mechanisms are the strategies and tools we employ to manage stress, bounce back from adversity, and maintain our emotional well-being. By consciously cultivating these coping mechanisms, we can build inner strength, enhance our ability to adapt, and thrive in the face of adversity.

One of the most powerful coping mechanisms for resilience is developing a strong support network. Surrounding ourselves with people who uplift, encourage, and understand us can provide a sense of comfort, validation, and perspective during difficult times. Whether it's family, friends, or a supportive community, having a network of individuals who can lend a listening ear, offer guidance, and provide emotional support can significantly bolster our resilience.

Another important coping mechanism is the practice of self-care. Taking care of our physical, emotional, and mental well-being is crucial for building resilience. This can involve engaging in activities that bring us joy and relaxation, such as exercise, hobbies, or spending time in nature. Additionally, prioritizing self-care activities like getting enough sleep, practicing mindfulness or meditation, and nurturing healthy relationships helps to recharge and strengthen our resilience in the face of challenges.

Cultivating a positive mindset is also a powerful coping mechanism for resilience. Adopting a mindset that focuses on growth, learning, and finding silver linings in difficult situations can help us maintain optimism and perseverance. By reframing negative thoughts into more positive and empowering narratives, we can navigate setbacks with resilience and develop a sense of inner strength.

Building coping mechanisms for resilience also involves developing effective problem-solving and stress-management skills. Learning to identify and address challenges head-on, breaking them down into manageable steps, and seeking solutions can help us feel more in control and empowered. Additionally, implementing stress-management techniques such as deep breathing, meditation, or engaging in activities that promote relaxation can help reduce stress levels and enhance our ability to handle adversity.

Cultivating emotional intelligence is another essential coping mechanism for resilience. Emotional intelligence involves understanding and managing our own emotions and effectively navigating social relationships. By developing skills in self-awareness, self-regulation, empathy, and effective communication, we can enhance our ability to navigate challenging situations, maintain healthy relationships, and bounce back from setbacks.

Flexibility and adaptability are also key coping mechanisms for resilience. Life is unpredictable, and being able to adapt to change and adjust our plans and expectations can help us navigate challenges with greater ease. Cultivating flexibility involves developing a growth mindset, being open to new possibilities, and embracing change as an opportunity for growth and learning.

In conclusion, developing coping mechanisms for resilience is an essential component of navigating life's challenges with strength, perseverance, and emotional well-being. Building a support network, practicing self-care, cultivating a positive mindset, developing problem-solving and stress-management skills, enhancing emotional intelligence, and embracing flexibility are all powerful tools for building resilience. By consciously engaging in these practices, we can develop the inner strength and resources to face adversity, bounce back from setbacks, and thrive in the face of life's challenges. Remember, resilience is not about avoiding difficulties, but rather about developing the tools and mindset to navigate them with strength, grace, and a belief in our own ability to overcome.

CHAPTER THREE

Embracing Failure as a Stepping Stone

RETHINKING FAILURE AS A LEARNING OPPORTUNITY

Failure is often seen as something to be feared and avoided at all costs. We are conditioned to believe that failure is a negative outcome, a reflection of our shortcomings or inadequacies. However, what if we shift our perspective and see failure as a valuable learning opportunity? What if we embrace failure as a catalyst for growth and resilience?

Rethinking failure begins with understanding that it is an inherent part of life's journey. No one is immune to failure; it is a shared human experience. When we reframe failure as a stepping stone rather than a stumbling block, we open ourselves up to new possibilities and a mindset of growth.

Failure provides us with invaluable lessons and insights. It is through failure that we learn about our limitations, areas for improvement, and what does not work. Each failure is an opportunity to gather information, adjust our approach, and refine our strategies. By embracing failure as a learning opportunity, we can become more resilient, adaptable, and ultimately, more successful.

Failure also teaches us important life lessons. It builds character, resilience, and perseverance. It teaches us humility and the importance of humility. When we fail, we are forced to confront our ego, face our fears, and develop a deeper understanding of ourselves. Failure pushes us out of our comfort zones and helps us grow as individuals.

One of the most significant benefits of rethinking failure is the liberation it brings. When we let go of the fear of failure, we are free to take risks, pursue our passions, and explore new avenues. We become more willing to experiment, innovate, and push the boundaries of what we believe is possible. Failure becomes a welcomed companion on our journey, guiding us towards our true potential.

To embrace failure as a learning opportunity, it is essential to adopt a growth mindset. A growth mindset recognizes that abilities and intelligence can be developed through dedication, effort, and learning from mistakes. It allows us to see failure as a temporary setback, rather than a permanent label. With a growth mindset, we become more resilient and optimistic, viewing failure as a necessary stepping stone on the path to success.

Rethinking failure also requires self-compassion. It is easy to be harsh and self-critical when we experience failure. However, treating ourselves with kindness and understanding allows us to bounce back and continue moving forward. By acknowledging our efforts, celebrating small wins, and offering ourselves grace, we build emotional resilience and maintain a healthy perspective on failure.

In the face of failure, it is crucial to surround ourselves with a supportive network. Having mentors, friends, or colleagues who can offer guidance, encouragement, and perspective can make a significant difference in our ability to learn from failure. They can provide insights, share their own experiences of failure, and help us navigate through challenging times. Together, we can create an environment that promotes growth and resilience.

Rethinking failure as a learning opportunity is a transformative mindset shift that empowers us to overcome obstacles, embrace challenges, and grow into our fullest potential. By reframing failure, we open ourselves up to a world of possibilities, resilience, and personal growth. So, let us not fear failure but welcome it as a valuable teacher on our journey towards success. Remember, the greatest achievements often arise from the lessons learned in the face of failure.

OVERCOMING FEAR OF FAILURE

Fear of failure is a common and powerful emotion that can hold us back from pursuing our dreams and reaching our full potential. It stems from the worry that we will fall short of expectations, face disappointment, or be judged by others. However, when we learn to overcome this fear, we open ourselves up to new opportunities, personal growth, and success.

One of the first steps in overcoming the fear of failure is to recognize that failure is a natural part of life. Every successful person has experienced failure at some point on their journey. It is through failure that we learn, grow, and develop resilience. By understanding that failure is not an endpoint but a stepping stone to success, we can begin to reframe our perception.

Another key to overcoming the fear of failure is to challenge our negative beliefs and self-doubt. Often, we create exaggerated scenarios in our minds, imagining the worst possible outcomes. However, these scenarios are rarely realistic. By questioning our negative thoughts and replacing them with more positive and realistic ones, we can diminish the power of fear and gain a sense of control over our mindset.

Taking small steps and setting achievable goals can also help in overcoming the fear of failure. Breaking down our larger goals into smaller, manageable tasks allows us to build confidence and momentum. Each small success contributes to a sense of accomplishment and gradually reduces our fear of failure. By celebrating these incremental victories, we reinforce the belief in our abilities and develop a more positive mindset.

Another strategy to overcome the fear of failure is to reframe failure as an opportunity for growth and learning. Instead of viewing failure as a reflection of our worth or abilities, we can see it as a chance to gather valuable feedback, make adjustments, and improve our approach. By shifting our perspective, we can embrace failure as a necessary and valuable part of the learning process.

Seeking support from others can also be instrumental in overcoming the fear of failure. Talking about our fears and concerns with trusted friends, family, or mentors can provide valuable insights, encouragement, and a fresh perspective. Sharing our experiences with others who have faced similar challenges can remind us that we are not alone and that failure is a shared experience.

Taking calculated risks and stepping out of our comfort zones is another powerful way to overcome the fear of failure. When we push ourselves to try new things and embrace challenges, we expand our capabilities and build resilience. Each time we face and overcome a fear, we prove to ourselves that we are capable of handling difficult situations and that failure is not as devastating as we may have imagined.

Finally, practicing self-compassion and self-acceptance is crucial in overcoming the fear of failure. We are often our harshest critics, holding ourselves to impossibly high standards. By treating ourselves with kindness, understanding, and forgiveness, we create a supportive and nurturing environment for personal growth. Remembering that failure does not define our worth as individuals allows us to approach challenges with greater courage and resilience.

Overcoming the fear of failure is not an overnight process but a journey of self-discovery and personal growth. It requires patience, perseverance, and a willingness to confront our fears head-on. By reframing our perception of failure, seeking support, taking risks, and practicing self-compassion, we can gradually diminish the power of fear and step into our true potential. Remember, failure is not something to be feared but an opportunity for growth, learning, and ultimately, success.

HARNESSING FAILURE FOR PERSONAL AND PROFESSIONAL GROWTH

Failure is often perceived as a setback, a disappointment, or even a source of shame. It is something most people try to avoid at all costs. However, failure is not an endpoint but a valuable opportunity for personal and professional growth. By harnessing the lessons within failure, we can unlock new insights, develop resilience, and propel ourselves forward towards success.

One of the key ways to harness failure for growth is through reflection and analysis. When faced with failure, taking the time to examine what went wrong, what could have been done differently, and what lessons can be learned is essential. This introspection allows us to identify patterns, uncover underlying issues, and make adjustments for future endeavors. By understanding the root causes of failure, we can develop strategies to prevent similar mistakes in the future.

Failure also provides an opportunity to build resilience. When we experience setbacks or disappointments, it tests our ability to bounce back and persevere. Each failure we encounter strengthens our resilience muscle, allowing us to navigate challenges with greater ease and determination. Embracing failure as a chance to grow stronger, we can face future obstacles with a renewed sense of confidence and perseverance.

Failure can also foster a growth mindset, a belief that abilities and intelligence can be developed through dedication and effort. When we view failure as a stepping stone towards improvement rather than a reflection of our abilities, we open ourselves up to new possibilities. We become more willing to take risks, learn from our mistakes, and push beyond our comfort zones. By embracing a growth mindset, we transform failure into a catalyst for personal and professional growth.

Another way to harness failure for growth is through reframing our perception of success. Society often glorifies success and tends to overlook the journey of failures and setbacks that often precedes it. By recognizing that failure is an integral part of the path to success, we can shift our focus from the end result to the process itself. Each failure becomes a stepping stone, an opportunity to learn, adapt, and refine our approach. With this mindset, we become more resilient, adaptable, and open to growth.

Failure also encourages creativity and innovation. When our initial plans or strategies fail, we are forced to think outside the box, explore alternative solutions, and take risks. Failure pushes us to embrace new perspectives, challenge conventional thinking, and seek innovative approaches. Some of the greatest inventions, discoveries, and breakthroughs have emerged from moments of failure. By embracing failure as an invitation to think differently, we unlock our creative potential and pave the way for groundbreaking ideas.

Lastly, harnessing failure for growth requires self-compassion and a healthy perspective. It is important to remember that failure does not define our worth as individuals. It is a natural part of the learning process and a necessary step towards success. Practicing self-compassion allows us to acknowledge our failures without self-judgment or harsh criticism. It enables us to treat ourselves with kindness and understanding, fostering a nurturing environment for growth and learning.

In conclusion, failure is not the end but a beginning— an opportunity for personal and professional growth. By harnessing the lessons within failure, reflecting on our experiences, building resilience, embracing a growth mindset, reframing our perception of success, fostering creativity, and practicing self-compassion, we can transform failure into a powerful catalyst for growth. Embracing failure as a teacher and a stepping stone, we unlock our true potential and pave the way for greater achievements and fulfillment in our lives.

CHAPTER FOUR

Finding Strength in Vulnerability

EMBRACING VULNERABILITY AS A SOURCE OF AUTHENTICITY

Vulnerability is often seen as a weakness, something to be avoided or hidden away. However, embracing vulnerability can be a powerful tool for cultivating authenticity and deepening connections with others. When we allow ourselves to be vulnerable, we show up as our true selves, with all our imperfections and insecurities. We open the door to genuine connections, personal growth, and meaningful experiences.

Authenticity is about being true to ourselves, expressing our thoughts, feelings, and experiences without pretense or masks. It is about embracing our uniqueness and owning our stories, even if they are messy or imperfect. Vulnerability is the gateway to authenticity. By embracing vulnerability, we let go of the fear of judgment and rejection, allowing others to see us as we truly are.

When we are vulnerable, we create space for genuine connections with others. It is through vulnerability that we build trust and intimacy in relationships. By sharing our vulnerabilities, we invite others to do the same, fostering a deeper level of understanding and empathy. We discover that we are not alone in our struggles and that our shared experiences can bring us closer together.

Embracing vulnerability also paves the way for personal growth and self-discovery. It takes courage to acknowledge and confront our fears, insecurities, and shortcomings. By allowing ourselves to be vulnerable, we create an environment of self-acceptance and self-compassion. We learn to embrace all parts of ourselves, including the parts we may consider imperfect or flawed. This acceptance enables us to grow, evolve, and become the best version of ourselves.

Furthermore, vulnerability opens doors to new experiences and opportunities. When we are willing to step out of our comfort zones and take risks, we invite growth and transformation into our lives. We become open to new possibilities, adventures, and learning experiences. By embracing vulnerability, we expand our horizons and embrace a life rich in meaningful moments and deep connections.

Being vulnerable also allows us to cultivate resilience. When we are open and honest about our struggles, setbacks, and failures, we demonstrate strength and resilience in the face of adversity. We show that we are not defined by our challenges but by how we respond to them. Through vulnerability, we find the courage to get back up, learn from our experiences, and keep moving forward.

Embracing vulnerability as a source of authenticity requires self-compassion and self-acceptance. It means letting go of the need for perfection and embracing our humanity. It is about acknowledging that vulnerability is a natural part of the human experience and that it does not diminish our worth or value. Instead, vulnerability allows us to connect with others on a deeper level, to embrace our authentic selves, and to live a life aligned with our true values.

In conclusion, embracing vulnerability as a source of authenticity is a transformative journey. It allows us to show up as our true selves, to connect with others on a deeper level, and to cultivate personal growth and resilience. By embracing vulnerability, we unlock the power of authenticity and create a life filled with meaningful connections, personal fulfillment, and a deep sense of self-acceptance. So, let go of the fear, embrace your vulnerabilities, and discover the transformative power of being real.

CULTIVATING SELF-COMPASSION AND SELF-ACCEPTANCE

In a world that often emphasizes achievement, comparison, and perfection, cultivating self-compassion and self-acceptance is a transformative act of kindness towards ourselves. It is about embracing our authentic selves, acknowledging our worthiness, and offering ourselves unconditional love and understanding.

Self-compassion is the practice of treating ourselves with the same kindness, care, and compassion that we would extend to a dear friend. It involves recognizing our own suffering, acknowledging our struggles, and responding with warmth and understanding. Instead of harsh self-criticism, self-compassion allows us to offer ourselves comfort, encouragement, and forgiveness.

Self-acceptance is the act of embracing all aspects of ourselves, both the positive and the challenging. It is about recognizing and honoring our strengths, talents, and accomplishments, while also acknowledging our limitations, mistakes, and imperfections. Self-acceptance means embracing our whole selves, without judgment or the need for external validation.

Cultivating self-compassion and self-acceptance is a lifelong journey, requiring patience, practice, and a shift in perspective. Here are some key principles and practices that can help us in this transformative process:

- Mindful Awareness: Developing self-compassion and self-acceptance starts with cultivating mindful awareness of our thoughts, emotions, and experiences. By tuning into our inner world, we can observe our self-critical thoughts, challenging emotions, and patterns of self-judgment. This awareness allows us to respond with kindness and understanding.

- Self-Kindness: Practice treating yourself with kindness and understanding, just as you would treat a beloved friend. When faced with difficulties or setbacks, offer yourself words of comfort, encouragement, and support. Replace self-criticism with self-compassionate and uplifting thoughts. Remember, you deserve love and kindness, especially from yourself.

- Common Humanity: Recognize that suffering, challenges, and imperfections are part of the shared human experience. No one is perfect, and we all encounter struggles along the way. Understanding that you are not alone in your experiences can help you cultivate self-compassion and realize that your worthiness is not contingent on perfection or external validation.

- Letting Go of Comparison: Release the habit of comparing yourself to others. Remember that each person's journey is unique, and everyone has their own set of strengths and challenges. Instead of comparing, focus on your own growth, progress, and self-improvement. Celebrate your own achievements and honor your own path.

- Self-Acceptance: Embrace your authentic self, including your strengths, weaknesses, and quirks. Recognize that self-acceptance does not mean complacency or lack of growth. It means acknowledging where you are in the present moment while actively working towards personal growth and development.

- Forgiveness: Practice forgiveness towards yourself for past mistakes, regrets, and perceived shortcomings. Let go of self-blame and self-judgment, and instead, offer yourself forgiveness and compassion. Remember that making mistakes is an essential part of learning and growth.

- Gratitude and Self-Celebration: Cultivate a sense of gratitude for yourself and your journey. Take time to celebrate your accomplishments, no matter how small. Focus on your strengths, talents, and positive qualities. Recognize the progress you have made and the resilience you have shown.

By cultivating self-compassion and self-acceptance, we create a foundation of inner strength, resilience, and well-being. We learn to embrace our authentic selves, to treat ourselves with kindness and understanding, and to navigate life's challenges with grace and compassion.

NURTURING RELATIONSHIPS AND SEEKING SUPPORT

Human beings are inherently social creatures. We thrive on connections and relationships that bring meaning, support, and fulfillment to our lives. Nurturing relationships and seeking support is not only essential for our well-being but also plays a crucial role in our personal and professional growth.

In today's fast-paced world, it's easy to become caught up in our own busy lives and overlook the importance of fostering meaningful connections. However, investing time and energy into building and nurturing relationships can have a profound impact on our overall happiness and success.

Here are some key reasons why nurturing relationships and seeking support is vital:

- Emotional Support: Building strong connections with family, friends, and loved ones provides us with a network of emotional support. These relationships offer a safe space to share our joys, sorrows, and challenges, providing comfort, empathy, and understanding. Having someone to lean on during difficult times can be immensely reassuring and can help us navigate through life's ups and downs.

- Networking and Collaboration: Cultivating relationships within our professional spheres opens doors to new opportunities, collaborations, and growth. Networking allows us to expand our knowledge, exchange ideas, and learn from others' experiences. It can lead to partnerships, mentorship opportunities, and access to valuable resources that can enhance our personal and professional development.

- Accountability and Motivation: Surrounding ourselves with supportive individuals can help us stay accountable to our goals and aspirations. By sharing our dreams and ambitions with trusted friends or mentors, we invite their encouragement, guidance, and gentle nudges when needed. These relationships can provide the motivation and accountability necessary to overcome obstacles and stay focused on our path.

- Different Perspectives and Feedback: Building relationships with individuals from diverse backgrounds and perspectives exposes us to new ideas, insights, and ways of thinking. Seeking feedback and input from trusted peers or mentors can offer valuable perspectives on our work, helping us refine our ideas, enhance our skills, and challenge our assumptions. This constructive feedback fosters personal and professional growth.

- Collaboration and Supportive Communities: Engaging with like-minded individuals who share our interests, passions, or professional goals can create a sense of belonging and camaraderie. Joining communities, attending workshops or conferences, or participating in online forums provides opportunities for collaboration, support, and mutual growth. These communities can be a source of inspiration, advice, and encouragement.

- Personal Growth and Empowerment: Nurturing relationships and seeking support empower us to recognize and harness our strengths, talents, and potential. Positive and supportive connections can boost our self-esteem, foster self-belief, and provide the encouragement we need to take risks, pursue our passions, and overcome self-doubt. By surrounding ourselves with individuals who believe in us, we are more likely to believe in ourselves.

- Fulfillment and Well-being: Meaningful relationships and a strong support network contribute to our overall sense of fulfillment and well-being. When we feel connected, supported, and valued, we experience a greater sense of happiness, purpose, and contentment. These relationships provide a sense of belonging and enrich our lives in ways that money or material possessions cannot.

Nurturing relationships and seeking support require effort, time, and genuine care. It involves being present for others, actively listening, offering support, and reciprocating kindness. It also means being open to vulnerability, allowing ourselves to receive help and guidance when needed.

In the journey of personal and professional growth, we must recognize the power of connections and actively nurture relationships. By surrounding ourselves with supportive individuals, seeking guidance, and fostering collaboration, we create a fertile ground for our own growth, happiness, and success.

CHAPTER FIVE

Transforming Setbacks into Success

OVERCOMING SETBACKS AND OBSTACLES

Life is full of twists and turns, and along our journey, we inevitably encounter setbacks and obstacles that test our resilience and determination. These challenges can come in various forms, such as failure, rejection, unexpected circumstances, or personal struggles. However, it is how we respond to these setbacks that shapes our growth, character, and eventual success.

Here are some key insights and strategies for overcoming setbacks and obstacles:

- Embrace a Growth Mindset: Adopting a growth mindset is essential when facing setbacks. Instead of viewing failures as permanent or personal flaws, see them as opportunities for growth and learning. Embrace the belief that challenges can be overcome through effort, perseverance, and continuous improvement. A growth mindset empowers you to see setbacks as temporary setbacks, not as defining moments.

- Reframe Setbacks as Learning Experiences: Every setback carries valuable lessons and insights. Take the time to reflect on what went wrong and identify areas for improvement. Ask yourself: What can I learn from this experience? How can I use this setback as an opportunity to grow and develop? By reframing setbacks as learning experiences, you transform them into stepping stones towards future success.

- Cultivate Resilience: Resilience is the ability to bounce back from setbacks and adapt to new circumstances. Cultivate resilience by developing effective coping mechanisms, such as practicing self-care, seeking support from loved ones, and maintaining a positive outlook. Remember that resilience is not about never experiencing difficulties; it's about bouncing back stronger and wiser from them.

- Break Down Goals into Manageable Steps: When faced with a daunting obstacle, it can be helpful to break it down into smaller, more manageable steps. This approach allows you to tackle one challenge at a time, building momentum and confidence along the way. By focusing on incremental progress, you can overcome even the most significant obstacles.

- Seek Support and Collaboration: Don't be afraid to ask for help or seek guidance from others. Surround yourself with a supportive network of friends, mentors, or professionals who can offer advice, encouragement, and a fresh perspective. Collaboration and shared experiences can provide valuable insights and emotional support during challenging times.

- Stay Flexible and Adapt: Sometimes, setbacks require us to shift our plans or approach. Be willing to adapt and make necessary adjustments to your strategies. Being flexible allows you to navigate obstacles more effectively and explore alternative paths to success. Remember, the ability to adapt is a strength, not a weakness.

- Maintain a Positive Mindset: Positivity and optimism can go a long way in overcoming setbacks. While it's natural to feel disappointed or discouraged initially, strive to maintain a positive mindset. Focus on the lessons learned, the progress made, and the possibilities that lie ahead. A positive outlook can help you persevere and find creative solutions to overcome obstacles.

- Celebrate Small Wins: Recognize and celebrate your achievements along the way, no matter how small they may seem. Celebrating small wins boosts your motivation, confidence, and resilience. Acknowledge the progress you've made, the lessons you've learned, and the strengths you've developed. By celebrating small victories, you build momentum and keep moving forward.

- Practice Self-Compassion: During challenging times, it's crucial to be kind and compassionate towards yourself. Avoid self-blame or negative self-talk. Treat yourself with the same kindness and understanding you would offer a friend facing similar setbacks. Practice self-care, engage in activities that bring you joy, and prioritize your well-being.

- Persevere with Determination: Remember that setbacks are not the end of the road; they are merely detours on your journey to success. Maintain a sense of determination and perseverance.

ADAPTING TO CHANGE AND BOUNCING BACK

In today's fast-paced and ever-changing world, the ability to adapt to change and bounce back from adversity is crucial for personal and professional success. Change is inevitable, whether it's in our careers, relationships, or life circumstances. Adapting to change requires resilience, flexibility, and a growth mindset that empowers us to embrace new opportunities and overcome challenges. By cultivating the skills and mindset necessary to navigate change, we can not only survive but thrive in the face of uncertainty.

Here are some key insights and strategies for adapting to change and bouncing back:

- Embrace Change as an Opportunity: Instead of resisting change or viewing it as a threat, shift your perspective and see it as an opportunity for growth and transformation. Recognize that change often brings new possibilities, experiences, and lessons. Embracing change with an open mind allows you to explore uncharted territories and discover hidden potential within yourself.

- Cultivate Resilience: Resilience is the ability to adapt and bounce back from setbacks. It is a fundamental skill that enables us to navigate change effectively. Cultivate resilience by developing coping mechanisms, practicing self-care, and maintaining a positive mindset. Remember that setbacks and challenges are part of the journey, and your resilience will help you overcome them.

- Stay Flexible and Agile: Rigidity can hinder our ability to adapt to change. Cultivate flexibility and agility by being open to new ideas, perspectives, and approaches. Be willing to adjust your plans, strategies, or goals when necessary. The ability to pivot and embrace new directions is crucial in a rapidly evolving world.

- Focus on What You Can Control: In times of change, it's essential to focus on what you can control rather than getting overwhelmed by external factors. Direct your energy and attention towards aspects of the situation that you can influence. This empowers you to take proactive steps and make intentional choices to navigate the change effectively.

- Seek Opportunities for Learning and Growth: Change often presents opportunities for learning and personal growth. Approach change with a mindset of curiosity and continuous improvement. Seek out new knowledge, skills, or experiences that align with the changing landscape. By embracing learning and growth, you equip yourself with the tools to adapt and thrive.

- Develop a Supportive Network: Surround yourself with a supportive network of friends, mentors, or colleagues who can provide guidance, encouragement, and perspective during times of change. Share your experiences, concerns, and aspirations with them. Their support can provide valuable insights, emotional support, and a sense of camaraderie.

- Practice Self-Reflection: Take time for self-reflection to gain clarity on your values, goals, and aspirations. Regularly assess your strengths, weaknesses, and areas for growth. This self-awareness will guide you in adapting to change in alignment with your core values and aspirations.

- Cultivate Emotional Intelligence: Emotional intelligence is the ability to recognize and manage your emotions and empathize with others. It plays a crucial role in navigating change effectively. Cultivate emotional intelligence by developing self-awareness, self-regulation, social awareness, and relationship management skills. These skills will help you navigate change with empathy, adaptability, and effective communication.

- Practice Mindfulness: Mindfulness is the practice of being fully present in the current moment, without judgment. It can help you stay grounded, reduce stress, and enhance your ability to adapt to change. By practicing mindfulness, you can cultivate a sense of calmness and clarity, enabling you to respond to change with greater ease and resilience.

- Celebrate Your Progress: Acknowledge and celebrate your progress as you navigate change. Even small steps forward deserve recognition and celebration.

CREATING A ROADMAP FOR SUCCESS

Success means different things to different people. It can be pursuing a fulfilling career, nurturing meaningful relationships, achieving personal growth, or making a positive impact in the world. Whatever your definition of success may be, creating a roadmap is essential to turn your dreams into achievable goals. A roadmap provides a clear direction, helps you stay focused, and guides you through the necessary steps to reach your desired destination.

Here are some key insights and strategies for creating a roadmap for success:

- Define Your Vision: Start by defining your vision of success. What does success mean to you? Visualize your desired future and articulate your aspirations, both personally and professionally. Having a clear vision serves as a guiding light and motivates you to stay committed to your goals.

- Set SMART Goals: Break down your vision into specific, measurable, attainable, relevant, and time-bound (SMART) goals. SMART goals provide clarity and structure, making them easier to plan and achieve. Ensure that your goals are realistic and aligned with your values, passions, and capabilities.

- Prioritize Your Goals: Not all goals are created equal. Prioritize your goals based on their importance and relevance to your overall vision. Identify the goals that will have the most significant impact on your success and focus your energy and resources on them. This allows you to allocate your time and effort effectively.

- Create Actionable Steps: Break down each goal into actionable steps or milestones. These steps outline the specific tasks, resources, and timelines required to achieve your goals. Breaking them into manageable chunks makes them less overwhelming and helps you track your progress along the way.

- • Develop a Plan: Create a comprehensive plan that outlines the sequence of actions required to achieve each goal. Identify the resources, skills, and support needed for each step. Set deadlines and create a timeline to keep yourself accountable. A well-structured plan provides a roadmap that keeps you on track towards success.

- Seek Knowledge and Skills: Identify the knowledge and skills required to achieve your goals. Invest in continuous learning, whether through formal education, workshops, seminars, or self-study. Acquiring new knowledge and skills enhances your competence and equips you with the tools needed to overcome challenges and seize opportunities.

- Cultivate a Growth Mindset: Adopt a growth mindset that embraces challenges, sees failures as learning opportunities, and believes in the power of effort and perseverance. Embrace the belief that your abilities and intelligence can be developed through dedication and hard work. A growth mindset allows you to stay resilient, adapt to obstacles, and keep moving forward.

- Monitor and Evaluate Progress: Regularly monitor and evaluate your progress towards your goals. Assess what is working well and what needs adjustment. Celebrate your achievements and milestones along the way to stay motivated. If necessary, revise your plan and make course corrections to stay aligned with your vision.

- Stay Persistent and Resilient: Success rarely comes without setbacks and obstacles. Stay persistent and resilient in the face of challenges. Maintain focus on your goals, even when progress seems slow or obstacles arise. Believe in your ability to overcome difficulties and persevere on your journey.

- Cultivate Balance and Well-being: Success is not only about achieving goals; it's also about maintaining balance and well-being in all aspects of your life. Prioritize self-care, nurture your relationships, and create space for activities that bring you joy and fulfillment. A well-rounded approach to success ensures long-term happiness and satisfaction.

Creating a roadmap for success requires self-reflection, goal-setting, planning, and consistent action. It empowers you to navigate your journey with clarity, focus, and resilience. Remember, success is a journey, and the roadmap you create will guide you towards your destination while allowing room for flexibility and adaptation along the way.

CHAPTER SIX

Cultivating Inner Strength and Self-Belief

BUILDING SELF-CONFIDENCE AND SELF-ESTEEM

Self-confidence and self-esteem are essential qualities that contribute to personal growth, happiness, and success. They shape how we perceive ourselves, how we interact with others, and how we navigate through life's challenges. Building and nurturing self-confidence and self-esteem is a lifelong journey that requires self-awareness, self-acceptance, and deliberate practice. By investing in these qualities, we empower ourselves to pursue our dreams, overcome obstacles, and live a fulfilling life.

Here are some key insights and strategies for building self-confidence and self-esteem:

- Challenge Negative Self-Talk: Become aware of your inner dialogue and challenge negative self-talk. Replace self-critical thoughts with positive affirmations and encouraging statements. Focus on your strengths, accomplishments, and unique qualities. By changing your self-talk, you shift your mindset to one of self-empowerment and positivity.

- Set Realistic Goals: Set goals that are challenging yet attainable. Break them down into smaller, manageable steps. As you achieve these milestones, your self-confidence grows. Celebrate your achievements, regardless of how big or small they may be. Each success reinforces your belief in your abilities.

- Celebrate Your Strengths: Recognize and appreciate your strengths and talents. Identify what you excel at and leverage those strengths in various aspects of your life. Embrace your uniqueness and the value you bring to the world. Celebrating your strengths builds a solid foundation for self-confidence.

- Step Out of Your Comfort Zone: Growth and self-confidence lie just beyond your comfort zone. Push yourself to take on new challenges, try new experiences, and embrace uncertainty. Each time you step out of your comfort zone and succeed, your self-esteem expands. Embrace the mindset of continuous growth and embrace new opportunities for self-discovery.

- Practice Self-Compassion: Treat yourself with kindness, compassion, and understanding. Embrace self-compassion by acknowledging that making mistakes and facing setbacks are part of the human experience. Offer yourself the same empathy and support you would give to a friend. Self-compassion allows you to bounce back from failures and setbacks with resilience.

- Surround Yourself with Supportive People: Surround yourself with positive, supportive individuals who believe in you and your potential. Seek out relationships with people who uplift and encourage you. Their belief in you can inspire self-confidence and provide a supportive environment for personal growth.

- Take Care of Your Physical and Mental Well-being: Nurturing your physical and mental well-being is crucial for building self-confidence and self-esteem. Engage in regular exercise, eat a balanced diet, and get enough sleep. Practice stress management techniques, such as mindfulness or meditation. When you prioritize self-care, you feel more energized, focused, and self-assured.

- Embrace Failure as a Learning Opportunity: Shift your perception of failure from a negative outcome to a learning opportunity. Understand that failure is not a reflection of your worth, but rather a stepping stone towards growth and improvement. Learn from your failures, adapt your approach, and persevere. Each failure becomes a valuable lesson that strengthens your self-confidence and resilience.

- Practice Assertiveness: Develop assertiveness skills to express your thoughts, feelings, and needs in a respectful manner. Set healthy boundaries and learn to say no when necessary. Assertiveness empowers you to advocate for yourself, assert your opinions, and take control of your life, enhancing your self-esteem.

- Celebrate Self-Improvement: Engage in activities that promote personal development and self-improvement. Continuously seek opportunities to learn, acquire new skills, and broaden your knowledge. When you invest in your personal growth, you build a sense of mastery and accomplishment, fueling self-confidence and self-esteem.

HARNESSING THE POWER OF POSITIVE AFFIRMATIONS

Positive affirmations are powerful tools that can transform your mindset, boost self-confidence, and cultivate a positive outlook on life. They are statements or declarations that are intentionally designed to counter negative thoughts, beliefs, or self-talk. By incorporating positive affirmations into your daily routine, you can rewire your thinking patterns, overcome self-doubt, and unleash your full potential. Harnessing the power of positive affirmations can lead to profound personal growth and empowerment.

Here are some key insights and strategies for harnessing the power of positive affirmations:

- Identify Limiting Beliefs: Start by identifying any limiting beliefs or negative self-talk that holds you back. Pay attention to recurring thoughts or statements that undermine your self-confidence or hinder your progress. Common examples include "I'm not good enough," "I always fail," or "I can't do it." Awareness is the first step in challenging and transforming these beliefs.

- Create Positive Affirmations: Once you've identified your limiting beliefs, craft positive affirmations that counteract them. Formulate affirmations that are positive, present tense, and personalized to your specific needs and goals. For example, if you struggle with self-doubt, an affirmation could be "I am capable and deserving of success in all areas of my life." Write down your affirmations and keep them in a visible place.

- Repeat and Reinforce: Regularly repeat your affirmations to reinforce their positive messages. Incorporate them into your daily routine, such as reciting them in the morning, during meditation, or before important tasks or challenges. Consistency is key, so make it a habit to consciously repeat and internalize your affirmations.

- Visualize and Feel the Affirmations: As you recite your affirmations, engage your imagination and visualize yourself embodying the qualities or achievements stated in the affirmations. Imagine the positive outcomes and the emotions associated with them. Visualizing and feeling the affirmations help to deepen their impact on your subconscious mind.

- Believe in the Affirmations: Develop a genuine belief in the affirmations you create. Trust that they reflect your true potential and align with your values and aspirations. Embrace them with conviction and conviction, even if you initially feel some resistance. As you consistently reinforce the positive messages, your belief in them will strengthen.

- Practice Self-Compassion: In addition to positive affirmations, practice self-compassion and kindness towards yourself. Treat yourself with understanding and forgiveness when you face setbacks or challenges. Remember that personal growth is a journey, and progress takes time. Embrace self-compassion as an integral part of your affirmation practice.

- Customize and Adapt: Tailor your affirmations to specific areas of your life where you seek growth or transformation. Whether it's career, relationships, health, or personal development, create affirmations that resonate with your desired outcomes in those areas. Customize and adapt your affirmations as your goals evolve or as you encounter new opportunities.

- Surround Yourself with Positivity: Create an environment that supports positive affirmations. Surround yourself with uplifting people, inspiring books, motivational quotes, and affirmations that resonate with your values and aspirations. Cultivate a positive atmosphere that reinforces your affirmations and nurtures your growth mindset.

- Journaling and Reflection: Use journaling as a tool to reflect on your affirmations, record your progress, and explore any insights or transformations that occur. Write down your thoughts, observations, and experiences related to your affirmations. Journaling provides a space for self-reflection and deepens your connection with your affirmations.

CULTIVATING A STRONG SENSE OF SELF-WORTH

A strong sense of self-worth is a fundamental pillar of personal well-being, confidence, and fulfillment. It is the belief that you are inherently valuable, deserving of love, respect, and happiness. Cultivating a strong sense of self-worth is a transformative journey that requires self-acceptance, self-compassion, and a deep understanding of your own worthiness. When you embrace your inherent value, you empower yourself to make choices that align with your authentic self and live a life of purpose and fulfillment.

Here are some key insights and strategies for cultivating a strong sense of self-worth:

- Practice Self-Acceptance: Embrace yourself fully, including your strengths, weaknesses, flaws, and imperfections. Recognize that being human means having both positive and negative aspects. Practice self-acceptance by letting go of self-judgment and embracing your authentic self. Acceptance is the foundation for building self-worth.

- Challenge Comparison and Perfectionism: Avoid comparing yourself to others, as it undermines your self-worth. Recognize that everyone has their own unique journey and strengths. Embrace the idea that you are enough just as you are, without needing to be perfect. Embrace self-compassion and focus on your own progress rather than external standards.

- Identify and Celebrate Your Strengths: Take time to reflect on your strengths, talents, and achievements. Acknowledge your positive qualities and the contributions you make in various aspects of your life. Celebrate your accomplishments, regardless of how big or small they may be. Recognizing your strengths enhances your self-worth and builds a positive self-image.

- Set Boundaries: Establishing healthy boundaries is crucial for cultivating self-worth. Learn to say no to activities, situations, or relationships that do not align with your values or well-being. Prioritize your needs and respect your personal limits. Setting boundaries communicates to yourself and others that you value and respect yourself.

- Practice Self-Compassion: Treat yourself with kindness, understanding, and self-compassion. Embrace the fact that making mistakes and facing setbacks are part of the human experience. Offer yourself the same empathy and support you would give to a loved one. Practice self-compassion during challenging times, allowing yourself to learn and grow from difficulties.

- Surround Yourself with Positive Influences: Surround yourself with people who uplift and support you. Seek relationships that are nurturing, positive, and respectful. Distance yourself from individuals who undermine your self-worth or bring negativity into your life. Surrounding yourself with positive influences fosters an environment conducive to self-worth cultivation.

- Practice Mindfulness and Self-Reflection: Engage in mindfulness practices that help you stay present and connected to your inner self. Regular self-reflection allows you to gain insight into your thoughts, emotions, and behaviors. Use this awareness to challenge negative self-talk and replace it with positive affirmations that reinforce your self-worth.

- Cultivate Healthy Self-Care Habits: Prioritize self-care activities that nourish your mind, body, and soul. Engage in activities that promote physical well-being, such as exercise, proper nutrition, and adequate rest. Take time for activities that bring you joy, relaxation, and rejuvenation. Self-care enhances self-worth by sending the message that you value and prioritize your well-being.

- Seek Growth and Learning: Cultivate a growth mindset and embrace opportunities for personal growth and learning. Set goals that challenge you and provide opportunities for self-improvement. Embrace new experiences, acquire new skills, and expand your knowledge. Each step toward growth reinforces your sense of worthiness and personal development.

CHAPTER SEVEN

Embracing Change and Reinvention

EMBRACING THE INEVITABILITY OF CHANGE

Change is an intrinsic part of life. From the smallest everyday occurrences to major life events, change is constantly shaping our experiences and shaping who we are. Embracing the inevitability of change is a vital skill that allows us to navigate life's transformative journey with resilience and adaptability. By accepting and embracing change, we open ourselves up to new possibilities, personal growth, and a deeper understanding of ourselves and the world around us.

Here are some key insights and strategies for embracing the inevitability of change:

- Recognize the Nature of Change: Understand that change is a natural and universal process. Just as the seasons change and the tides ebb and flow, our lives are in a constant state of flux. Accepting this truth helps us let go of resistance and embrace the opportunities that change brings.

- Embrace Uncertainty: Change often brings uncertainty, and that can be uncomfortable. However, it is important to embrace the unknown and see it as an opportunity for growth and discovery. View uncertainty as a gateway to new experiences and possibilities, rather than something to fear or avoid.

- Foster a Growth Mindset: Cultivate a growth mindset, which is the belief that we can learn, adapt, and grow through any situation. See change as an opportunity for personal development and expansion. Embrace challenges as learning experiences and approach them with curiosity and a willingness to learn.

- Practice Flexibility and Adaptability: Develop the ability to be flexible and adapt to new circumstances. Recognize that rigid expectations and attachments can hinder our ability to navigate change effectively. Embrace a mindset of adaptability and be open to adjusting your plans and perspectives when needed.

- Let Go of Resistance: Resistance to change often stems from fear of the unknown or the discomfort of leaving our comfort zones. By letting go of resistance, we free ourselves from unnecessary suffering and open ourselves up to the possibilities that change brings. Embrace the idea that change is an opportunity for growth and transformation.

- Seek Opportunities for Learning and Growth: Embrace change as a catalyst for learning and personal growth. Take advantage of new experiences, challenges, and opportunities that arise from change. Approach them with curiosity and a willingness to learn, and you will discover new strengths and capabilities within yourself.

- Practice Self-Reflection: Engage in regular self-reflection to gain insight into your reactions and emotions regarding change. Reflect on how past changes have shaped you and what lessons you have learned. Use this self-awareness to develop strategies for effectively navigating future changes.

- Build Resilience: Resilience is the ability to bounce back from adversity and adapt to change. Cultivate resilience by building a strong support network, practicing self-care, and developing coping mechanisms for stress and uncertainty. Enhancing your resilience will empower you to face change with confidence and bounce back from challenges.

- Embrace Change as an Opportunity for Reinvention: Change provides us with the chance to reinvent ourselves and explore new possibilities. Use change as a catalyst for self-discovery and personal transformation. Take the opportunity to reassess your goals, values, and priorities and make any necessary adjustments.

- Find Meaning and Purpose: Embrace change by seeking meaning and purpose in each phase of your journey. Reflect on how change contributes to your personal growth, relationships, and overall well-being. By finding meaning in the midst of change, you can navigate through it with a sense of direction and clarity.

In conclusion, change is an inevitable part of life. Embracing the inevitability of change allows us to navigate life's journey with resilience, adaptability, and a sense of purpose.

NAVIGATING LIFE TRANSITIONS WITH GRACE

Life is a series of transitions. From graduating college to changing careers, from starting a family to entering retirement, we constantly find ourselves navigating through different stages and chapters of our lives. These transitions can be both exciting and challenging, requiring us to adapt, grow, and find balance amidst change. Navigating life transitions with grace involves embracing the journey, cultivating resilience, and approaching change with intentionality and self-care.

Here are some key insights and strategies for navigating life transitions with grace:

- Embrace the Process: Recognize that transitions are a natural part of life's evolution. Embrace the idea that change brings new opportunities for personal growth and self-discovery. Instead of resisting or fearing transitions, choose to approach them with curiosity and openness. Embracing the process allows you to navigate transitions with greater ease and grace.

- Cultivate Resilience: Develop resilience as you navigate life's transitions. Resilience is the ability to bounce back from adversity and adapt to new circumstances. Build your resilience by practicing self-care, seeking support from loved ones, and maintaining a positive mindset. Resilience provides a solid foundation for managing the challenges that often accompany life transitions.

- Set Realistic Expectations: Be realistic about what to expect during transitions. Understand that transitions may involve periods of uncertainty, adjustment, and emotional ups and downs. Avoid placing undue pressure on yourself to have everything figured out immediately. Set realistic expectations and allow yourself the time and space to navigate the transition at your own pace.

- Seek Support: Reach out to your support network during life transitions. Share your feelings, concerns, and goals with trusted friends, family members, or mentors. Seek guidance and advice from those who have gone through similar experiences. Surrounding yourself with supportive individuals provides a sense of reassurance and encouragement during times of change.

- Practice Self-Care: Prioritize self-care throughout the transition process. Take care of your physical, emotional, and mental well-being. Engage in activities that bring you joy, relaxation, and rejuvenation. Nurture your body through exercise, healthy eating, and sufficient rest. Self-care helps you maintain balance and resilience during life transitions.

- Reflect and Reassess: Use life transitions as an opportunity for self-reflection and reassessment. Take the time to evaluate your values, goals, and aspirations. Consider if the transition aligns with your authentic self and if any adjustments or changes need to be made. Reflecting and reassessing allows you to navigate transitions with intentionality and purpose.

- Embrace the Unknown: Transitions often involve stepping into the unknown. Embrace the uncertainty and view it as an opportunity for personal growth and discovery. Embracing the unknown requires a willingness to be open to new experiences, ideas, and perspectives. Trust in your abilities to adapt and learn as you navigate through unfamiliar territory.

- Practice Mindfulness: Incorporate mindfulness into your daily life to navigate transitions with grace. Be fully present in the moment, acknowledging and accepting your thoughts and emotions without judgment. Mindfulness helps you cultivate a sense of calm and clarity, allowing you to make conscious choices and navigate transitions with greater awareness.

- Celebrate Milestones and Progress: Recognize and celebrate milestones and achievements along the way. Acknowledge the progress you have made, no matter how small it may seem. Celebrating milestones boosts your confidence, reinforces your resilience, and motivates you to keep moving forward.

- Practice Gratitude: Cultivate gratitude for the journey, including both the challenges and the joys that come with life transitions. Appreciate the lessons learned, the growth experienced, and the opportunities that arise. Gratitude fosters a positive mindset and helps you maintain perspective throughout the transition process. When you practice gratitude, you shift your focus from what may be uncertain or challenging to what you are grateful for in your life. This shift in perspective allows you to see the silver linings, the lessons, and the blessings that come with each transition.

REDISCOVERING PASSION AND PURPOSE

Passion and purpose are driving forces that give meaning and fulfillment to our lives. They ignite our inner flame, fuel our motivation, and guide us towards a life of significance. However, there are times when we may feel disconnected from our passion and lose sight of our purpose. Rediscovering passion and purpose is a transformative journey of self-exploration, introspection, and aligning our actions with our authentic selves.

Here are some key insights and strategies for rediscovering passion and purpose:

- Reflect on Your Values and Priorities: Begin by reflecting on your core values and priorities. What matters most to you? What principles and beliefs shape your decisions and actions? Aligning your life with your values is a crucial step in rediscovering passion and purpose. It allows you to live in accordance with your authentic self.

- Explore Your Interests and Curiosities: Engage in activities that spark your curiosity and bring you joy. Take time to explore different hobbies, interests, and passions. Allow yourself to be curious and open to new experiences. Pay attention to what activities energize you and make you feel alive. Rediscovering passion often involves trying new things and stepping out of your comfort zone.

- Reconnect with Childhood Dreams: Revisit your childhood dreams and aspirations. Reflect on what excited you as a child and the activities that brought you joy and fulfillment. Often, our childhood dreams hold valuable clues about our true passions and purpose. Reconnecting with those dreams can reignite the flame within and inspire a new direction.

- Seek Inspiration from Others: Surround yourself with people who inspire and uplift you. Seek out mentors, role models, or individuals who have found their passion and purpose. Learn from their experiences and seek guidance and support. Engaging with inspiring individuals can help spark new ideas, perspectives, and possibilities.

- Step Out of Your Comfort Zone: Rediscovering passion and purpose often requires stepping out of your comfort zone. Embrace new challenges and take calculated risks. Push yourself to try things you've always wanted to do but were hesitant to pursue. Growth and self-discovery happen when we stretch beyond our limits.

- Engage in Self-Reflection: Take time for self-reflection and introspection. Journaling, meditation, or quiet contemplation can help you gain clarity about your passions and purpose. Reflect on your strengths, values, and the impact you want to make in the world. Self-reflection allows you to connect with your inner self and listen to your intuition.

- Find Meaning in Service: Serving others can be a powerful way to rediscover passion and purpose. Consider how your unique talents and abilities can contribute to the well-being of others. Engaging in acts of kindness, volunteering, or pursuing a career that makes a positive impact can ignite a sense of purpose and fulfillment.

- Embrace Continuous Learning: Cultivate a growth mindset and a thirst for knowledge. Embrace opportunities for learning and personal development. Take courses, attend workshops, read books, or seek mentorship. Continuous learning expands your horizons, exposes you to new ideas, and helps you discover new passions and interests.

- Set Goals and Take Action: Once you've identified your passion and purpose, set goals that align with your aspirations. Break them down into actionable steps and create a plan of action. Take consistent and intentional steps towards your goals, knowing that each small action contributes to the greater picture. Remember, progress is a journey, and taking action is essential for rediscovering passion and purpose.

- Practice Self-Compassion: Be kind and patient with yourself throughout the process of rediscovery. Embrace the ups and downs, the detours, and the uncertainties. Practicing self-compassion is a vital component of rediscovering passion and purpose. It involves treating yourself with kindness, understanding, and acceptance, especially during times of uncertainty or when faced with challenges.

CHAPTER EIGHT

Living a Balanced and Fulfilling Life

PRIORITIZING SELF-CARE AND WELL-BEING

In the hustle and bustle of our daily lives, it's easy to overlook our own well-being. We often prioritize work, responsibilities, and the needs of others, leaving little time and energy for ourselves. However, prioritizing self-care and well-being is essential for maintaining a balanced and fulfilling life. It involves taking intentional steps to nurture your physical, mental, and emotional health. By making self-care a priority, you can enhance your overall well-being and live a more vibrant and meaningful life.

Here are some key insights and strategies for prioritizing self-care and well-being:

- Recognize the Importance of Self-Care: Understand that self-care is not selfish or indulgent; it is a necessary act of self-preservation. Just as you would care for a loved one, it is crucial to prioritize your own well-being.

When you take care of yourself, you have more energy, resilience, and capacity to show up fully in other areas of your life.

- Assess Your Needs: Start by assessing your needs across various domains of well-being, including physical, mental, emotional, and spiritual aspects. What areas of your life require attention and nourishment? Identifying your needs will help you develop a personalized self-care plan.

- Establish Boundaries: Set healthy boundaries to protect your time, energy, and overall well-being. Learn to say no to activities or commitments that drain you or don't align with your priorities. Prioritize activities that bring you joy, relaxation, and fulfillment.

- Practice Mindful Awareness: Cultivate mindful awareness by being fully present in the present moment. Pay attention to your thoughts, emotions, and physical sensations without judgment. Mindfulness helps you tune into your needs and make conscious choices that support your well-being.

- Nourish Your Body: Take care of your physical health by prioritizing healthy habits. Eat a balanced diet, stay hydrated, engage in regular exercise, and get sufficient sleep. Nourishing your body with wholesome foods, movement, and rest enhances your energy levels and overall vitality.

- Nurture Your Mind: Engage in activities that stimulate and nurture your mind. Read books, explore new hobbies, engage in creative pursuits, or engage in intellectually stimulating conversations. Continuously challenging and expanding your mind contributes to your overall well-being.

- Cultivate Emotional Well-being: Pay attention to your emotional needs and develop strategies to support your emotional well-being. Practice self-compassion, engage in activities that bring you joy, connect with loved ones, and seek professional support when needed. Prioritizing emotional well-being allows you to navigate life's challenges with resilience and grace.

- Connect with Nature: Spend time in nature and connect with the natural world. Nature has a calming and rejuvenating effect on our well-being. Take walks in the park, go hiking, or simply sit and observe the beauty of nature. Connecting with nature restores a sense of balance and provides a valuable respite from the demands of daily life.

- Engage in Activities That Bring Joy: Identify activities that bring you joy, passion, and a sense of purpose. It could be anything from playing a musical instrument, painting, dancing, gardening, or volunteering. Engaging in activities that ignite your inner spark replenishes your energy and nurtures your soul.

- Practice Self-Compassion: Be kind and gentle with yourself. Treat yourself with the same compassion and understanding you would offer to a dear friend. Embrace your imperfections, celebrate your strengths, and forgive yourself for mistakes or shortcomings. Self-compassion cultivates a positive and nurturing relationship with yourself.

STRIKING A BALANCE BETWEEN WORK, RELATIONSHIPS, AND PERSONAL GROWTH

In our fast-paced and demanding world, finding balance among work, relationships, and personal growth can be a significant challenge. Often, we find ourselves pouring all our energy into one area while neglecting others, leading to feelings of overwhelm, burnout, or dissatisfaction. Striking a balance between these crucial aspects of life is essential for overall well-being and a fulfilling existence. It involves intentional choices, effective time management, and nurturing each area to create harmony in our lives.

Here are some key insights and strategies for striking a balance between work, relationships, and personal growth:

- Clarify Your Priorities: Start by clarifying your priorities and values. What truly matters to you? Identify the areas that are most important in your life, such as career success, meaningful relationships, personal growth, health, or leisure. Understanding your priorities helps you allocate time and energy accordingly.

- Set Boundaries: Establish healthy boundaries to create space and time for each aspect of your life. Clearly define your working hours and communicate them to colleagues and loved ones. Set aside dedicated time for personal growth activities, quality time with family and friends, and self-care. Boundaries help prevent one area from overpowering others.

- Practice Effective Time Management: Develop effective time management strategies to optimize your productivity and create a balanced schedule. Prioritize tasks and allocate specific time blocks for work, relationships, and personal growth activities. Use tools like calendars, to-do lists, or time-tracking apps to help you stay organized and make the most of your time.

- Honor Quality over Quantity: Focus on the quality of your time rather than the quantity. It's not about how much time you spend in each area but how present and engaged you are during that time. Whether it's work, spending time with loved ones, or pursuing personal growth, be fully present and give your undivided attention.

- Practice Effective Communication: Open and honest communication is vital in maintaining balance. Communicate your needs, boundaries, and expectations to colleagues, family members, and friends. Seek understanding and collaboration to find mutually beneficial solutions that support work-life integration and personal growth.

- Foster Supportive Relationships: Cultivate supportive relationships that understand and respect your need for balance. Surround yourself with individuals who support your personal and professional growth, and who understand the importance of nurturing all aspects of your life. These relationships provide the encouragement and understanding needed to strike a balance effectively.

- Develop Self-Awareness: Cultivate self-awareness to recognize when one aspect of your life is dominating the others. Pay attention to your thoughts, emotions, and physical sensations to identify signs of imbalance. Regularly check in with yourself to assess whether you are giving enough attention to work, relationships, and personal growth.

- Create Boundaries around Technology: In today's digital age, technology often blurs the boundaries between work, personal life, and relationships. Establish boundaries around technology use to prevent it from encroaching on your personal time. Set aside designated "tech-free" times or spaces to fully engage with loved ones and prioritize personal growth activities.

- Prioritize Self-Care: Self-care is crucial for maintaining balance and overall well-being. Make self-care a non-negotiable part of your routine. Schedule time for activities that rejuvenate and replenish you, such as exercise, meditation, hobbies, or relaxation. Taking care of yourself allows you to show up fully in your work and relationships.

- Embrace Flexibility and Adaptability: Recognize that balance is not a static state but a dynamic process that requires flexibility and adaptability. Life circumstances and priorities may shift over time, and it's important to adjust your focus and approach accordingly. Embrace the idea that balance is not about dividing your time equally between work, relationships, and personal growth, but rather finding harmony and satisfaction in the integration of these areas.

FINDING JOY AND FULFILLMENT IN EVERYDAY LIFE

In our pursuit of happiness, we often overlook the simple joys and experiences that can bring immense fulfillment to our lives. We may find ourselves constantly chasing after future goals or dwelling on past regrets, missing out on the beauty and opportunities that exist in the present moment. However, finding joy and fulfillment in everyday life is not about extraordinary events or grand achievements; it's about cultivating a mindset of gratitude, presence, and embracing the small moments that bring us joy. Here are some key insights and strategies for finding joy and fulfillment in everyday life:

- Practice Gratitude: Cultivate an attitude of gratitude by consciously acknowledging and appreciating the blessings and joys in your life. Take time each day to reflect on the things you are grateful for, whether it's a beautiful sunset, a kind gesture from a friend, or a moment of laughter. Gratitude shifts your focus towards abundance and amplifies the positive aspects of your life.

- Be Present: Embrace the power of the present moment. Practice mindfulness and fully engage in whatever you are doing, whether it's having a conversation, enjoying a meal, or walking in nature. Notice the sensory details, savor the experiences, and let go of distractions. Being present allows you to fully experience the richness and beauty of each moment.

- Cultivate Mindful Habits: Incorporate mindful habits into your daily routine. It could be starting your day with a few minutes of meditation or mindfulness exercises, taking mindful walks in nature, or practicing mindful eating. These habits help you slow down, connect with yourself and the world around you, and find joy in the simplicity of everyday activities.

- Find Meaning in Everyday Tasks: Infuse meaning into your everyday tasks by connecting them to your values and purpose. Whether it's doing household chores, completing work assignments, or running errands, approach them with intention and a sense of purpose. Recognize the importance of these tasks in creating a harmonious and fulfilling life.

- Engage in Activities that Bring Joy: Identify activities that bring you joy and make time for them regularly. It could be playing a musical instrument, painting, dancing, gardening, or reading a book. Engaging in activities that align with your passions and interests nourishes your soul and brings a sense of fulfillment.

- Practice Random Acts of Kindness: Spread joy by practicing random acts of kindness. Extend a helping hand to someone in need, offer a kind word or gesture, or surprise a loved one with a thoughtful act. Acts of kindness not only bring happiness to others but also enhance your own sense of purpose and fulfillment.

- Foster Meaningful Connections: Nurture meaningful connections with loved ones, friends, and your community. Invest time and energy in building and maintaining relationships that bring you joy, support, and connection. Engage in meaningful conversations, create memories together, and celebrate the beauty of human connection.

- Embrace Nature: Spend time in nature and appreciate its beauty and serenity. Whether it's taking a hike, having a picnic in the park, or simply sitting in your backyard, immersing yourself in nature allows you to find peace, rejuvenation, and a deeper connection with the world around you.

- Practice Self-Care: Prioritize self-care and make time for activities that nourish your well-being. It could be taking a bubble bath, practicing yoga or meditation, enjoying a hobby, or engaging in self-reflection. Taking care of yourself ensures that you have the energy and emotional balance to fully embrace the joys of everyday life.

- Embrace Imperfection: Let go of the pursuit of perfection and embrace the beauty of imperfection. Life is full of ups and downs, and it's okay to embrace the imperfections and challenges that come along. Accepting that life is a mix of highs and lows allows you to find joy and fulfillment even in the face of adversity.

Embracing Your Journey of Falling and Flailing

Life is a journey filled with unpredictable twists and turns, successes and failures, and moments of pure joy and profound sadness. It's a journey where we often find ourselves falling and flailing, facing challenges and setbacks that test our resilience and strength. However, it is in these moments of falling and flailing that we have the opportunity to grow, learn, and discover our true selves.

Throughout this journey, we have explored various aspects of personal growth, self-compassion, relationships, resilience, and self-discovery. We have learned that success is not a destination but a continuous process, and setbacks and obstacles are merely stepping stones on the path to growth and fulfillment.

Embracing your journey of falling and flailing requires a shift in mindset, a willingness to accept and embrace the inevitable ups and downs of life. It is about letting go of the fear of failure and seeing it as an opportunity for growth and self-discovery. It's understanding that setbacks are not a reflection of your worth but a chance to learn, adapt, and bounce back stronger than before.

In this journey, cultivating self-compassion and self-acceptance is crucial. It's about treating yourself with kindness and understanding, embracing your flaws and imperfections, and recognizing that you are worthy of love and respect, regardless of the challenges you face. Self-compassion allows you to navigate through difficult times with grace and resilience, and it becomes the foundation for building self-confidence and self-esteem.

Nurturing relationships and seeking support are vital in our journey of falling and flailing. Surrounding yourself with a supportive network of loved ones who believe in you, celebrate your successes, and lift you up during difficult times provides a sense of belonging and strength. It's about fostering authentic connections and being vulnerable enough to ask for help when needed. Together, we can overcome obstacles and find solace in the collective support of those who genuinely care.

Adapting to change and bouncing back are essential skills to embrace on this journey. Life is dynamic, and change is inevitable. Embracing change allows us to let go of what no longer serves us, explore new possibilities, and adapt to different circumstances. It's about finding resilience within ourselves, learning from our experiences, and using them as stepping stones to move forward.

Creating a roadmap for success provides direction and clarity, but it's important to remember that success is not a linear path. The roadmap should allow for flexibility, room for growth, and unexpected detours. It's about setting goals and intentions while remaining open to the opportunities and possibilities that present themselves along the way.

Building self-confidence and self-esteem is a continuous process rooted in self-belief and self-empowerment. Investing in personal growth, celebrating your achievements, and embracing your unique qualities and strengths contribute to building a strong sense of self-worth. It's about acknowledging that you have the power to create the life you desire and pursuing your passions with unwavering determination.

Harnessing the power of positive affirmations and cultivating a strong sense of self-worth are tools that empower us on this journey. Positive affirmations are powerful statements that reinforce positive beliefs and thoughts, helping to overcome self-doubt and foster a positive mindset. Embracing a strong sense of self-worth means valuing yourself, honoring your needs and boundaries, and pursuing a life that aligns with your values and aspirations.

Navigating life transitions with grace is an art that requires adaptability, resilience, and a willingness to embrace the unknown. Life transitions can be challenging and unsettling, but they also offer opportunities for growth and self-discovery. It's about finding the balance between letting go of the past and embracing the possibilities of the future, all while staying grounded in the present moment.

Embracing Change and Transformation

In this additional material for the book "Falling or Be Flailing: Embracing Your Journey of Growth and Resilience," we explore the transformative power of change and the importance of embracing personal growth with resilience and determination. Through practical advice, inspiring stories, and insightful reflections, this chapter guides readers on a path of self-discovery and transformation.

UNDERSTANDING THE NATURE OF CHANGE

- *Embracing the Inevitability of Change:* Change is an inherent part of life, and resisting it only leads to frustration and stagnation. By accepting the inevitability of change, we can develop the resilience and adaptability necessary to navigate life's twists and turns.

- *Recognizing the Opportunities in Change:* Change often brings new possibilities and opportunities for growth.

By reframing our perspective and viewing change as a chance for personal development, we can harness its potential and embrace the transformative journey it offers.

- *Letting Go of Fear and Control:* Fear and the desire for control can hinder our ability to embrace change. By cultivating a mindset of openness, surrender, and trust, we can free ourselves from the grip of fear and allow change to unfold naturally.

- *Cultivating a Growth Mindset:* Adopting a growth mindset enables us to view challenges as opportunities for learning and personal development. By seeing setbacks as stepping stones and embracing a belief in our own capacity to grow, we can navigate change with optimism and resilience.

THE JOURNEY OF SELF-DISCOVERY

- *Exploring Personal Values and Purpose:* Self-discovery begins with introspection and an exploration of our core values and passions. By aligning our actions with our authentic selves, we can uncover our true purpose and live a more fulfilling life.

- *Embracing Self-Reflection and Mindfulness:* Self-reflection and mindfulness practices foster a deeper understanding of our thoughts, emotions, and desires. Through these practices, we can cultivate self-awareness, gain clarity, and make conscious choices aligned with our values.

- *Overcoming Self-Limiting Beliefs:* Negative self-beliefs can hold us back from reaching our full potential. By challenging and reframing these limiting beliefs, we can unlock new possibilities, build self-confidence, and embark on a journey of self-empowerment.

- *Embracing Vulnerability and Authenticity:* Embracing vulnerability and embracing our authentic selves is essential for personal growth. By embracing our imperfections and being true to who we are, we create space for genuine connections, meaningful relationships, and personal transformation.

BUILDING RESILIENCE AND EMOTIONAL WELL-BEING

- *Cultivating Resilience in the Face of Challenges:* Resilience is the ability to bounce back from adversity. By developing coping strategies, fostering a positive mindset, and nurturing a strong support network, we can navigate life's challenges with strength and grace.

- *Emotional Intelligence and Self-Care:* Emotional intelligence involves understanding and managing our own emotions effectively. By practicing self-care, emotional regulation, and cultivating healthy coping mechanisms, we can enhance our emotional well-being and build resilience in the face of adversity.

- *Building Healthy Relationships:* Healthy relationships are vital for personal growth and well-being. By fostering open communication, empathy, and mutual respect, we create a supportive network that nurtures our growth and resilience.

- *Cultivating Gratitude and Finding Meaning:* Gratitude and finding meaning in our experiences can transform our perspective on life. By cultivating a gratitude practice, seeking purpose in our actions, and finding joy in the present moment, we can enhance our well-being and build resilience.

EMBRACING CHANGE AS A CATALYST FOR PERSONAL GROWTH

- *Setting Goals and Taking Action:* Embracing change involves setting meaningful goals and taking intentional action. By defining clear objectives, creating action plans, and staying committed to our growth journey, we can make tangible progress towards our desired outcomes.

- *Embracing Uncertainty and Adaptability:* Change often comes with uncertainty, and adapting to new circumstances is crucial. By cultivating flexibility, embracing the unknown, and viewing challenges as opportunities for growth, we can navigate change with resilience and grace.

- *Celebrating Milestones and Acknowledging Progress:* Celebrating milestones, no matter how small, is essential for motivation and self-appreciation. By acknowledging our progress and rewarding ourselves along the journey, we fuel our motivation and sustain our commitment to personal growth.

- *Cultivating Self-Compassion:* Self-compassion is the foundation for embracing change and fostering personal growth. By treating ourselves with kindness, understanding our inherent worth, and practicing self-acceptance, we can navigate challenges with resilience, grace, and a deep sense of self-love.

EMBRACING THE JOURNEY OF GROWTH AND RESILIENCE

The journey of personal growth and resilience is not a linear path but a transformative adventure. By embracing change, embarking on a journey of self-discovery, building resilience, and welcoming personal growth, we unlock our true potential and create a life of purpose, fulfillment, and authenticity. Through every challenge and triumph, we evolve into the best versions of ourselves, living a life of meaning and embracing the boundless possibilities that lie ahead.

A LIFELONG COMMITMENT

The journey of growth and resilience is an ongoing commitment that continues to unfold throughout our lives. It requires dedication, self-reflection, and the willingness to embrace change. As we continue on this path, we discover that our ability to embrace change and nurture personal growth is the key to living a life of purpose, resilience, and true fulfillment.

A LETTER TO THE READER

It is with great excitement and a touch of vulnerability that I present to you "Falling or Be Flailing," a heartfelt exploration of life's challenges, setbacks, and failures, and the extraordinary opportunity they present for growth and transformation. Within these pages, I invite you to embark on a journey of self-discovery, resilience, and personal empowerment—a journey that will redefine your perspective on failure and enable you to embrace the fullness of your potential.

Life is a beautiful and complex tapestry of experiences. It is a series of triumphs and tribulations, moments of elation and moments of defeat. We often find ourselves navigating the ebb and flow of life, searching for meaning, purpose, and a sense of direction. Yet, it is during our most challenging moments—the times when we stumble, fall, and flail—that we have the opportunity to rise and become our most authentic selves.

"Falling or Be Flailing" is an invitation to reframe our perception of failure, to embrace vulnerability, and to cultivate the resilience necessary to navigate life's inevitable obstacles. It is a reminder that setbacks are not setbacks at all but rather stepping stones on the path to personal growth and self-discovery. It is a testament to the strength that resides within each of us—a strength that may lay dormant until we face adversity head-on.

Within these pages, you will find a collection of heartfelt stories, reflective exercises, and practical strategies designed to help you navigate the complexities of life with grace, courage, and resilience. Drawing upon my own experiences and the wisdom of others, I offer insights and guidance on how to overcome fear, harness the power of vulnerability, and cultivate a positive mindset that will empower you to embrace the challenges that come your way.

Throughout this journey, you will discover that falling does not define you—it is how you choose to respond that matters most. It is in your response to life's challenges that you uncover your true strength, resilience, and ability to rise above any obstacle. It is in these moments of falling that you have the opportunity to become the most authentic version of yourself—to embrace your vulnerabilities and allow them to shape your character and your path forward.

I invite you to open your heart and mind as you embark on this transformative journey. Be willing to explore the depths of your emotions, the crevices of your fears, and the heights of your aspirations. Be open to the wisdom that lies within these pages, knowing that it is not a prescription for a perfect life but rather a roadmap for embracing the imperfections and using them as catalysts for growth.

Remember, you are not alone in your journey. We all stumble, fall, and flail at times, but it is through these experiences that we learn, grow, and become stronger. "Falling or Be Flailing" is a companion on your path—a guide that will walk beside you, offering solace, encouragement, and practical tools to help you navigate the inevitable ups and downs of life.

As you delve into the pages of this book, I encourage you to reflect upon your own experiences, to engage with the exercises and prompts provided, and to embrace the lessons that resonate with you. Take the time to sit with your emotions, to embrace vulnerability, and to celebrate the resilience that lies within you.

May "Falling or Be Flailing" be a source of inspiration, empowerment, and transformation. May it ignite a fire within you—a fire that fuels your courage, propels you forward, and reminds you of your inherent worthiness. May it serve as a reminder that falling is not a sign of weakness but a testament to your bravery in embracing life's challenges.

I am honored to join you on this journey of self-discovery and personal growth. Let us embark on a remarkable journey together, one that embraces the beauty of falling and rising with unwavering courage. Within the pages of "Falling or Be Flailing," we will delve into the depths of our experiences, exploring the transformative power that lies within moments of adversity and challenge.

Neeraj Sharma
Founder, Director & CEO
Authorland Self Publishing LLP

OUR LATEST
RELEASED BOOKS

कहाँ पहुँचे आप?

जीवात्मा जगत और 7 चक्रों की यात्रा के रहस्य

राजीव सक्सेना

The Author's Journey:
A Comprehensive Guide to Becoming an Author
YOUR DREAM Book
PLAN IT | PUBLISH IT | PROMOTE IT
BESTSELLER ON AMAZON
YOUR DREAM BOOK
THE AUTHOR'S JOURNEY: A COMPREHENSIVE GUIDE TO BECOMING AN AUTHOR
NEERAJ SHARMA

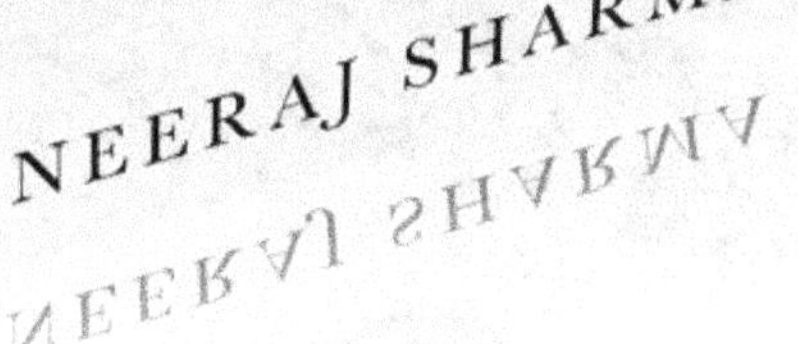
NEERAJ SHARMA

How to Write and Publish
YOUR OWN
BOOK
PRIYANKA "AABHAS"

कैसे लिखें कैसे छापें
आपकी अपनी
किताब
प्रियंका "आभास"

UNLOCKING THE SECRETS TO AUTHORSHIP AND FINANCIAL SUCCESS
PUBLISH YOUR BOOK AND MAKE MONEY
A COMPLETE GUIDE FOR COACHES, TRAINERS, CONSULTANTS, SPEAKERS, ENTREPRENEURS, STUDENTS AND EVERYONE WHO WANTS TO SELF-PUBLISH A BOOK AND MARKET IT
YUKTI SHARMA
PUBLISH YOUR BOOK AND MAKE MONEY
YUKTI SHARMA

A BRIEF RETOLD VERSION OF
TRUE INDIAN MYTHOLOGY
RAMAYANA
NEERAJ SHARMA
RAMAYANA
NEERAJ SHARMA

TOP SECRET ANCIENT
INDIAN SPIRITUAL KNOWLEDGE

UNLOCKING
The Secrets of
Breath

The
Ultimate
Life
Changer

Embark on a Journey of
Self-Discovery Through Breath

RAJEEV SAXENA

A GUIDE TO BECOMING AN
#1 NEW YORK TIMES BESTSELLER
THE ROAD TO
#1
Breaking #1 Bestseller Barriers
The Power of #1: Cracking the Code to Becoming a #1 Bestseller
DAKSH KAUSHIK
THE ROAD TO #1
DAKSH KAUSHIK

चक्रों को जाग्रत करने की संपूर्ण जानकारी और
साधना-विधियों की आसान गाइड

चक्र हीलिंग
चेंज योर लाइफ़

आपकी ऊर्जा शक्ति के 7 केंद्र

1 मूलाधार
2 स्वाधिष्ठान
3 मणिपूरक
4 अनाहत
5 विशुद्ध
6 आज्ञा
7 सहस्रार

बेस्टसेलर बुक
"लॉ ऑफ़ रहस्य"
के बेस्टसेलर लेखक

राजीव सक्सेना

www.ingramcontent.com/pod-product-compliance
Lightning Source LLC
LaVergne TN
LVHW010545200726

843506LV00013B/2930